old stone
&
between giants

Also by Ashley Capes and published by Ginninderra Press
7 Years (Pocket Poets)

ashley capes

old stone
&
between giants

Acknowledgements

Poems in this collection have previously appeared
in the following publications:
Modern Haibun and Tanka, *21D*, *Windmills*, *Verity LA*,
Haibun Today, *Speedpoets*, *Third Australian Haiku Anthology*,
Paper Wasp, *Shamrock*, *Heron's Nest*, *A Hundred Gourds*,
Contemporary Haibun Online, *World Haiku Review*,
Haiku Bandit Society, *Calico Cat Contest*, *Bluepepper*, *foam:e*, *Tincture*,
Prune Juice, *Acorn*, *Island*, *Going Down Swinging*, *fourW*, *dotdotdash*,
Cordite Poetry Review, *Colloquy*, *Stylus Poetry Journal*/*Another Lost Shark*,
Unusual Work, *Miscellaneous Voices: Australian Blog Writing*,
Black Rider Press (audio), *extempore*, *Famous Reporter*, *Windmills*,
Vibewire, *Queen Vic Knives*, *Block*, *Mascara Literary Review*, *P
AN Magazine*, *Wet Ink*, *Rex*,
Antipodes – A Global Journal of Australian/New Zealand Literature
and *Best Australian Poems 2012*.

I would like to thank the editors of the above publications for
their support and a big thanks especially to Stephen and Brenda
at Ginninderra Press.

old stone & between giants
ISBN 978 1 74027 949 9
old stone copyright © Ashley Capes 2014
between giants copyright © Ashley Capes 2012

old stone first published 2014
between giants first published 2012

This combined edition first published 2015 by
GINNINDERRA PRESS
PO Box 3461 Port Adelaide SA 5015
www.ginninderrapress.com.au

Contents

old stone	**9**
haiku & senryu	11
haibun	29
temple	31
Vatican Blues	32
shade cloth	33
weatherboarding	34
dovetails	35
each night	36
limoncello	37
senza	38
rooftop	39
a slow passage	40
from twelve to one	41
birthday	42
green skeletons	43
little wren	44
three months of imagining	45
night train	46
a grave turn	47
en route	48
Roman Forum (1)	49
Firenze	50
between giants	**51**
transitions	53
old green paint	54
birds still talking	55
southern autumn	56
not just you	57
capture	58
archaeological moment	59
Vesuvius sleeping	60
through the backyard	62

Keith Jarrett's scarecrow	63
stillness	64
now in the night	65
silver breadcrumbs	67
narrow beds	68
the sneaking moon	69
horse-drawn	70
hutchi street	71
stubble	72
a table set for thousands #2	73
pre-collapse confession	74
man of cloth	76
down from the sky	77
altitude blues	78
acceptance speech	79
jumped	80
a table set for thousands	81
concrete buttons	83
the colour purple	84
mythical	85
tiger-shells	87
things without beds	88
slow to get there	89
tv torch song	90
lemon-yellow waltz	91
stamped flat stamped	92
man about town	93
leather cocoon	95
windstorm	96
ridges in the skin	97
things get better	98
you steal a boat	99
a hunk of tomorrow	100
one of the townsfolk	102
particle detectors	104
snow	105

yellows	106
a ripening	107
twenty-thousand heartbeats	108
Saint Mark's Square	109

old stone

haiku & senryu

church steps
lead to a beggar's cup
sunburnt tourists

in the Botticelli room
crowds around
portable air conditioners

shuffling over old stone
the echo
of tour guides

shadows on the courthouse
shouting
over the pram

silver screen groans
stretched across
another romantic comedy

re-runs —
the police chief
is always balding

through the hiss
of long grass
a crane's careful walk

        this year
        instead of bushfire
        big dragonflies

                pushing memories
                along a dirt road
                wind

such orange –
nobody's flowers
on the roadside

not surprised
to see me again
chocolate shop

old ice on the sill
how once
we could laugh

through the shutters
a single fly
carries the chug of boats

Florence Haiku Sequence

blood orange
in small plastic cups
green fields blur

sidewalk café
crowded with the
swell of English accents

miniatures
in the souvenir shop
the fan droops

frozen white
David's hands
tower over us

trimming mat board
with borrowed scissors
Dr Conrad squirms

        wagons cut deep
        now only
        rain comes this way

                cameras jostle for position
                Pompeii plaster cast

an ache in my wrist
kids line up
their laptops

my poor finger!
a patch of skin
on the hotplate

thistles dance
autumn wind
muffles the highway

rough music –
brown beetle shells
underfoot

        grey thistles
        the rosella
        enthroned

                drying off
                the bathtub sings
                an awful song

you are trying to sleep
and I am Coltrane's sax
steeped in sound

first thing this morning
half a mouse
on the concrete

caught between
the passenger seat
fuel docket

the front carriage
becomes day-care
I slink into my book

        in a staring contest
        with the leaves
        green stick insect

                almost two a.m.
                dogs surprise each other
                between fences

night fishing –
two pelicans
just out of sync

big moon
I get the right key
first time

cosmic oven
even the bricks sparkle
tonight

reading a book
the ocean has been
on the same page forever

        chopping wood
        a cold wind
        across the field

                down beneath
                the toaster
                a raisin hides

a creak in my back –
the garden bed
mists over

watching the dogs
race leaves
afternoon sun

typing fast
a spring lullaby
on the roof

my back to the window
the sun's
thin fingers

        how the wind
        tries to sing
        old tin shed

                bench seat —
                just enough frost
                for a snowball

        watching us play
        the scarecrow's
        button-face

    the old bookshelf
    each spine reads
    welcome back

writing late
moths patter
against the glass

haibun

temple

Pompeii rains. its grey sky is mutated in cobblestones and wagon ruts glisten in the quiet. its stray dogs are patient, waiting for pizza. your runners look out of place. synthetic. flexible. I follow you to the brothel, where stone beds lurk in shadow. our guide jokingly describes the frescoes as 'menus'. the water has no memory. it is all in the earth. nothing is soft now

> filling with jackets
> and umbrellas
> temple ruins

Vatican Blues

at each bottle-necked corridor it's one step forward, two steps back. the tour groups are a mass of wandering cattle, linked by their brightly coloured transistors. they bump into us, rigid, processional, lacking a sense of purpose and trampling ghosts of the past. occasionally an arm steals above the din and at its top, like a star on a Christmas tree, is the unblinking eye of a camera. it makes its theft and retracts in shame

        sweat beads
        we stake out
        the open window

shade cloth

we ride our bikes everywhere and want sunburn for eventual tans that the girls will supposedly notice. no pale strips of winter-skin, no slip slop slap, no lectures from our doctors or parents. eventually more than the sun sinks in, and I begin duelling with thick globs of sunscreen. it will be the headline act next summer—that welcome grease, the hard-to-hold bottle, its smell mixing with the fabric in towels and the clean, clean sand

        diving from the rocks
        gold leaves spin
        on black water

weatherboarding

the first night is Chinese takeaway in a dining room
that we never eat in again. the fire is unlit, its patience
for winter is unbelievable. I unpack boxes of CDs and
place them in a contradictory mix of genres, decades
and even dates of purchase. you work on the kitchen
and cannot believe how stupid the cupboards are,
where the hell does the fridge go? in the half-gap we
place a brand-new clothes dryer, a white-goods knight
for the eternal damp of the valley

> *tre e trenta*
> an unfamiliar hum
> crosses the room

when streetlights blink out the last night is pulled over
my shoulders. I have cleaned the floors and walls,
the trollish oven, the windows muttering and cannot
find the strength to celebrate. the radio (later sold at
a garage sale) keeps good company, as the BBC sends
Noam Chomsky across heavy waves, until it is finally
switched off

> no ceiling fan
> overnight sweat
> sets on my skin

dovetails

the workshop bears the unmistakable scent of sawdust, one my father still carries home in his flannelette shirts. it migrates between us, invisible wings sparkling where the sun has tripped through Perspex skylights. buzzing saws mimic an angry hive. machined timber is smooth, the burrs stack themselves in mutated reds and browns. they lurk like sullen teenagers with hair in their eyes and plans in their pockets. later my father will soothe them into feature-pieces or small coasters, treat them for heat and our obsession with coffee. they will grow flat and still, have no more frowns

> not even a shadow on him
> my sweat
> follows the grain

each night

you and I work to feed our laptops. in return, we get
shovel-loads of fuzz and light from their Sauron-eyes.
we take trivia away and put our souls in. they blink as
we back them up. we snack. the temperature drops.
midnight slips by, you turn the tennis on. later, I won't
be able to dream

>	my wrist is a bear
>	on a mouse
>	it clicks and aches

limoncello

in the square we buy tea towels and chocolate spoons, stroll the market, pass lemon-themed shops, pass the mossy diorama in its fountain, go back down and photograph the church, see the hills, see the ocean, see through green shutters into someone's kitchen, sit and eat and drink, lemon cake and coffee perfect, pass cars and bikes and their horns beeping and moving pedestrians, passing the smell of petrol and cigarette smoke, steps and lines, the growling boats and street musicians, passing over money and putting cards into machines and waiting for the buses to clear and rain to stop

> still for a moment
> the sea breeze
> in your hair

senza

in Rome I could only steal the romance of silence.
every quiet postcard mocked me, pressed in at the
fountain by hands, bags and greedy eyes – yet my own
were mirrors

>a hundred cameras
>lined up
>coins flash

at sidewalk cafés time stretched so slow that even a
diet coke was something special and I know, it was
because you were there with me. a new rock, leading
where I took only small steps. how often we said
'we'll remember this' and we did. years later, I cling to
those three weeks

>standing at the sink
>picture books
>gather dust

rooftop

smog swallows the horizon. five storeys below, car horns start their hoarse arguments. the musician has enough rhythm tracks to last two nights, his keyboard is immune to the chatter. dinner arrives. Diana cigarettes are lit, pot plants turn black and the panna cotta wobbles, giving a hipless little dance before collapsing around my spoon

> carpeted walls
> no one speaks
> in the elevator

a slow passage

the airport announces itself in two voices, both
clipped, electronic manicure. harried faces pool at
terminals, they think only in numbers. a glow catches
in the fluid of their eyes and coffee's warm blush rises
above sweat and aftershave. I imagine one passenger
has shed the last twenty-four hours of a James Bond-
like life, bloodstained clothes exchanged for a black
forest suit and taxi fare

> in sweeps the wind
> leaves tickling
> our suitcases

with knives for teeth a child is at work on her parents.
newspapers are raised like inky shields. grunts are
issued. *toys now toys now chocolate now phone credit too
now that thing now this one mum, dad, please, now why
not now?* other people nap on red-cushioned chairs.
their jackets make for designer blankets and it's a
featherweight sleep, they know, at any moment could
come a summons to borrowed wings

> the point of your chin
> on my shoulder
> landing gears creak

from twelve to one

slow-moving windscreens bounce heat into the
gardens and the town centre is busy with people on
break. office folk and tradesmen fence with white and
orange clothing, waiting in queues for award-winning
pies to be handed out by teenagers with Facebook
smiles. on a bench seat, an abandoned water-bottle
crystallises sunlight, falling onto insects caught in
fresh lacquer. up where the stoplights have their fun,
taxis purr

> birdsong!
> buying a book with my
> first royalty cheque

birthday

fog is silvered by the sun. tears appear like rags on
a ghost. the river does not move but instead passes.
the trees stoop to agree, trailing their green fingers.
still the water swallows everything. not just fishing
line or starlight plucked from the sky, but the secrets
and dreams we whisper to ourselves as we glide by,
seat belts locked, windscreens thickening. white lines
curving

>	return trip
>	your toes
>	marking the glass

green skeletons

stems of new bracken are like the arms of green
skeletons, bursting from the earth and up into a
shock of hair. behind them, the older, brown ones
have put up their complex, dry latticework. across
a fallen trunk, moss roams like close-cropped afro.
green scents mesh with freshly hewn dirt; my shovel
uncovers grubs, almost nothing like their sugary
counterparts. I've pulled back their blanket of earth
and now they curl up tight, missing the dark

>resting on my handle
>even the fly
>wants some shade

little wren

sixteen steps to the gutter and the glitter of lost
change caught in a cage of yellow leaves all through
the afternoon crickets gossip their voices bright brittle
castanets exhaust fumes sneak over fences pass tiny
bones stuck in gardens at night moonlight plays an
empty bottle and wind brings you up the street turns
wheels

> on the roadside
> little wren
> a wise twitch

three months of imagining

in winter snow does not fall, crash or collect in
gutters, it does not come to rest between the litter and
buildings. it does not evoke a wonderland from where
such things are usually trapped within the electricity
of film and television, instead it makes you think of
rain on stone. instead, winter is a shortening of days
and a bloated heating bill, it is a frozen robin, it is ice
glinting on barbed wire, a mighty pastel that washes
green from the fields

>   new playground –
>   the wind has stopped
>   each voice

night train

the train chews at the city with the click and clack of
steel teeth, burrowing deeper to come face to face
with man-made black. we do not shiver and we do
not speak, unwilling to switch off long enough to
look around. the stations pass like flick-book pages;
yellow, orange, blue, white, red and bits of purple
too. some of us cannot wait. we're already standing,
feet ready to take us on a dance from platform
to platform, moving moving moving making the
shuffling music of panic

> so little room
> a woman's bra strap
> pressed against glass

a grave turn

streets have a saliva sheen. stones bathe in it. fog
is school-pants grey, thick on the tongue. the older
trams shudder until they stop and the conductor
retires. drunks smirk with red-balloon cheeks, dallying
through each step. it is a grave turn. they milk their
charm and spend it on ghosts in make-up, loosen
their teeth. a clean wind moves the leaves from side to
side, the clucking of winter within

> our snapshots –
> the photo booth
> becomes a grave marker

en route

the ultra cheerful sound of The Asteroids Galaxy
Tour chirps from the radio as our driver sets his
tanned hands on the wheel. his sleeves are rolled
up over the wrist, where a wealth of dark hair lives
like localised forest. he does not move his shoulders
much, but to roll them occasionally. twice he gestures
to the green range of Monte Cerreto, to tell us that
Amalfi is on the other side.

he does not mention the columns of smoke that pour
from different spots on the mountain, coloured slow.
they grow as if exhaled by dragons buried deep in the
earth, perhaps smuggled over Byzantine trade routes
from beyond the sea. we stare out the window, catch
glimpses of bright scales glittering on waves

>   narrow way –
>   black garbage bags
>   tied to fences

Roman Forum (1)

the spot where Caesar's body was burnt seems to
scare our guide. she does not look at the flowers and
waves at the mound, a sheen of sweat on her face as
the sun works its centuries-slow destruction on pillars
in the Forum

> uneven footing
> horns from
> the imperial road

up where the Vestal Virgins had their garden, rose
beds breathe easy. green pools might once have
hidden tears or swallowed sighs. of the many statues,
only two have heads and their creamy robes are mute.
people rest before them, hands on hips

> posing for photos
> other tourists
> fill the frame

Firenze

beneath the Duomo, cameras mill about like ants.
their owners are most dutiful, clicking then looking.
inside my skull are painted green and white stripes
and when I look back, it is with some terror. I do not
know if I wanted to go home. the air here is warm,
eternal pink, as if trapped in a fairy tale. the tourists
are so alive, even as they kill the moment with SLR

>grand bells
>cross the rooftops
>our hands meet
>between giants

between giants

transitions

the airport is a clone of another airport.
we are waved through.
our water is not.
a smile would tear the universe
into pebbles. it would hurt reputations.
I expect gas masks.
travelators make you want to run.
we sit. often, we are sitting
and eavesdropping through no fault of our own.
voices travel – we should be envious.
it is not always that clean.
people sleep in whatever shapes their bodies
fall into. it is a horrid jigsaw of seats and flesh.
tank tops. headdress. jeans designed to fade.
the boarding pass is grave, like communion bread.
announcements are goddess-like.
windows cover more square miles than football fields.
food is.
hands get shopping bag fatigue. ball and chain luggage.
money changes in a shallow register.
euros become american dollars become dirham
become australian. water is regained.
transfer signs bloom at baggage claims.
everything is duty-free.

old green paint

beneath the bridge
where the busker and his flute
compete with urine and the Yarra,
a schoolgirl drops change
into his case
and her friends giggle

down from the bridge
boats are lined up
like waterproofed hawkers,
no better at boasting than
old green paint on the staircase
or the predictable swish
of a waitress al fresco

and across the bridge
Flinders Street Station
lies sunbathing,
fake-tan yellow fading
and the rhythmic click of the train
becoming the wristwatch
of a patterned vein.

birds still talking

even this late, with the sun pedalling
downhill, birds are still talking
as warm bricks
leftover from noon
cook ants
and soothe the ache in my back,
watching the lid on the letter box
swing, click and squeak

I am taking hope seriously
in weather this good, no jumper
and no shoes –
it's getting better for walks
along the river after work,
when all the mind can manage
is little sounds of appreciation,
when words would
only cloud things over, burden
everything with meaning.

southern autumn

three witches jostle for position
above the bay of Naples,
breathing their smog-spells
across armoured water and into the hills

at Amalfi boats trudge in and out
to unburden themselves
of tourists
and with barely enough time
to sneak a drink, they're gone again

sunlight wakes short shorts
and thin singlets,
restaurants bustle
but no one is swimming and the bakery
has riddled away magic

on Cerreto's rigid slopes
lemons brave the wind,
their fragile gold shielded
by generations of latticework.

not just you

but a lover's camera
poses everything:

from the pack of Longbeach 20s
crushed into the stone wall

to the city-sanctioned fernery
with its green rattle of spring,

or the toddler with an inevitable
ice-cream grin

a bystander pointing out
landmarks

and the mass of school uniforms
bottled up at ATMs

– even the buildings lean
to get in shot.

capture

p i c a s s o
stood in big white blocks
in front of the gallery
and a pink hand
ran across his letters,
as the sun set between buildings

somewhere in the park
ghosts flitted from statue
to statue
and trams blocked
the road with steel smiles

while winter trees
had the sky in patches
and the pavement
navy blue

we sat and waited
for the 72
and Picasso's
'O' jumped out

I photographed the whole word:

a red light stopped the entire
street, and in the lower
curve of the 'S'
a man was caught, his
shopping bags glued to air.

archaeological moment

a penny has come thousands of miles
to hibernate in the dirt

it's not worth much
but neither is it worth nothing

once we clean it in a glass of coke
and the royal head has a nose again

we take it inside, though the first one
to tire of it reaches for the Sega

later on I don't know which one of us
will take it to the front shed

where the Nissan lords it over dead flies
that gather in the window sill,

and hide the penny behind a landscape
mum and dad haven't unpacked

years later when moving house
and neither one goes back for it

the penny can close its tiny eyes
to wait for a more archaeological moment.

Vesuvius sleeping

the pillow was a grill
and the band
down the street
sang to the ocean
fishing boats
bobbing along

her voice powering through
notes
boxing gloves on

we turned over
and it got hotter in the hotel
varnish on the shutters
snickered
and flies batted
their drowsy heads
against the glass

tomorrow we would need
to be awake
properly for Pompeii

to see the dogs
the deep wagon ruts
the stone brothel
and somehow
come to realise just how brutal
a volcano can be

but her voice echoed on
and our air conditioner
had been missing

since check-in
and my head was Crying
the Lot of 49
a half-finished
copy sitting beside
the semi-functional phone

and you weren't sleeping either

but neither of us
could bear to admit it
and so instead of talking
we lay there
and waited
for the mountains
to swallow up the last
of the music

scrape its bowl clean
with thunder
and hints of rain

through the backyard

in the hushed blue of the moon
you move bare feet
across concrete
still warm
as if just taken out
of some cosmic oven

little things make way;

>a bottle cap
>overturned like a turtle

>snail pellets
>bright with poison

>and smiling toys
>still posed by the flower bed

jasmine follows your skirt

as you drift from home to home
spinning clotheslines
and uncovering
strawberries
too young
to make a sound
when much later, the sun
climbs up and takes you back.

Keith Jarrett's scarecrow

his notes haunt the house
as I prepare to sleep, but it's ok. I like its echo
because I'm less alone
when listening in the black, having it broken
only
by strips of light
that slip in around the curtains,
that pour from streetlights
by the park, where the spider webs
wait for morning dew in rigid patterns
and cross walking paths
that I'll later cruise
in sandals that demand more pavement
and more summer.

I do not wake once he begins
and it might only be four minutes
before I'm dreaming
that single pillow in the middle of our bed
like a goodbye note,
wrapping my head softly
so all the disaster can bleed right out

and the whole time, the stereo stands across the hall,
turned down quite low
but with its little lights unblinking,
the perfect scarecrow for
bad dreams.

stillness

the funeral was incomprehensible.

children would not look around,
could not look at the coffin
slipping into the earth,
could not remember faces

only tall black pants
and the memory of a moustache,
dragging his mouth into a frown

unable to figure out the stillness
in a place so full of people,
unable to figure out
the promise of heaven
in such large bouquets, all the hand
shaking and the shaking that
went on from shoulders
once ideal for piggyback rides

and the son, his numb face spreading
across those gathered like a sure drug,
blanking out their voices.

now in the night

now in the night
                    peach
              with more sig
              nificance than a bible
      to a drunk
      minister
      mourning his dwindling flock
            in an age where
      Jesus is digitally
      encoded

              & no pew
                    can fit desk-chair-spines
                            or hearts with
wheels

      now in the night
      a chance at happiness
            just to hear rain
                  dancing on the roof
            partying

      magnificently, now in the night   a
hand
smooths hair
spread across pillows
      gone to porcelain

in wave after wave
of moonlight

                                                                            in
                &   now   the
                                                                            night

cutting up a banana
to chase away sugar-filled
        dreams
        & finding signs
                in loose change
                        or
                      a patt
                      ern seen
                        only when the sun
                            hits the curtains just right
we're both
looking for the same thing –
we're just strung out on different predictions

        both right down there
                on our knees
                when we think
no one is looking.

silver breadcrumbs

before the tennis courts
snails leave their jagged mess of silver breadcrumbs
but never turn back

they run the gauntlet

taking on the footpath chariots
the drunks and joggers
the small shoes of children
and broken glass

they block out the wider world
focus on the next centimetre

as tennis racquets
fire their dull gunshots
and the horizon burns
chimneys down to black

not a single twitch from their liquid eyes.

narrow beds

in the car park the air smells good;
shelves are being restocked
spills mopped
registers beeping and clicking
behind me,
as summer flowers linger
in narrow beds
set between heroic volumes of tar

across the road the post office
puffs its chest out,
old bricks covering up the sunset
and their edges going to gold

a few steps from the car
there's a familiar twinge of panic.
autumn is running out on me,
leaves settle between buildings
and trees undress
in a thin, worried dance –

when the cold comes
I will go home each night
and draw the curtains early.

the sneaking moon

I have missed the sneaking moon
these months
chaining myself to whatever desk
was at hand and emptying my head –
mass evacuation from a fleshy
and out-of-shape Titanic,
getting the letters out and dealing
with the dry ink of the keyboard,
its digital chicanery
its keystroke puppet show
its trouble director

and though the words spill out to batter
the emptiness between us
like oil-slick
Olympic sprinters,
they are little more than a sun-shower
on the mountainside,
its indifference majestic.

horse-drawn

in the square a couple
of horse-drawn tourists
gobble the sights
and I have to admit
I'm not too far behind them –
only I have no wheels
and the architecture seems to hush me
as much as they squawk

no matter that the locals
have long since tired
of my stuttering Italian
or my hunt for elusive music stores

the passage of strangers
as they sweep by
in their cover-shoot outfits
doesn't dampen my spirit

here such disinterest
is an eyelash to the wind,
candles light smiles
where they float in sidewalk cafés
and just the thought of pasta
warms me through.

hutchi street

when we're apart
I go looking for you
in the week we met

your green cardigan
and how sick that pizza made you
your notebooks
full of poems
photos and stories of ex-boyfriends

a long night
talking everything
everything and
tracing the spider-web-touch
of headlights against your walls

heading to 7/11
for crunchie ice cream
the next morning and coming across
your neighbour cutting his lawn
with scissors, our laughter
when we get back and close the door,
teeth still cold.

stubble

in *A Fistful of Dollars* Clint Eastwood's stubble
is thick enough to hide deer
or slow-witted
prospectors

an entire town could crop up
in the hollow of a cheek
with a village square
and a well
in the nick from a razor

and in the unlikely event of a smile

panic as the forest
sways.

a table set for thousands #2

I have to let the words make mistakes,
dozens of them, years of them
tonnes of them
before
I can take them out to dinner,
introduce them to dangerous types
happy holidays, marriage ceremonies
gainful employment, theft of history
blood feuds
strange cousins
and salesmen with coins that sparkle
like wishes in fountains,
before
I send them to gods with shaven heads
or bookies lined up, pads in hand
and travellers with shirts open
blouses, glimpses of skin
and bookkeepers
smirking in shadow
turning pages
sharing secrets with silverfish
and customers
eager to be invited
to a dance that leaves
ink stains in a tango
across the mind, eyes that blink back
an assault of meaning, jokes or
careless barbs
and claims that simply
cannot be true.

pre-collapse confession

you're right I'm talking too fast

a bouncy-ball
red

for her lipstick

and clouds covering the bay
in ultrasound green

once a fortnight

I make this gesture to the future

but somehow still end up
treating it

too much like a safety lap

the possibility of gentle envy
turns up in tea leaves

joyriding the pipes
beneath our kitchen sink

rich with old wives' truths

the hopelessness of manhood

a glass of water and two pills
safe
an actual
album of photos

last September was the best
of
our lives

ten years coming up
unmarked

man of cloth

somehow after you wear
my T-shirts
they seem softer,
smell better
and I don't want to take them back

being happy can be this simple
so I stand in the wardrobe
a little longer,
hold the cloth to my face.

down from the sky

the day bleeds out
all over the treetops
and the clouds make a fuss,
swooping low
to 'ooh' and 'aah' as they
patch up the wound

I'm standing by the tiny clothesline
and it's jetty of cement,
a square slab that just manages
to get it's chin above
the swell of grass

it's in this moment that I dare
to leave the house,
hope that a breeze
might have climbed down from the sky,
at last ready
to make up for such a long absence.

altitude blues

on the plane I read
to keep from thinking about
altitude

but the captain supplies his own distraction
as he flirts with each stewardess
over the loudspeaker,
presumably so we can all hear
how well
he straddles the line
between charming
and inappropriate

and while the girls smile
mid-demonstration
(life jackets, whistles
and lights in hand)
it seems that
quite quickly
Rachel's lipstick
becomes a thin line
and she forgets to sway back up the aisle.

acceptance speech

actually, while I'm here
I'd like to thank my dentist
for standing up to my recklessness,
even if the remorse
of the sugar-junkie never lasts

so I'd like to thank all the bakeries
and ice-creameries
from across the land too

and my mechanic
for going through all that grease
just to keep me mobile

I want to thank my bank, I suppose
because I'm renting
and can't tear up the floorboards
for that secret stash
in fact, I don't even have floorboards

and I can see I'm really running overtime now
so one more thing –
I want to thank my dry cleaner
because my favourite jacket
is always so clean
and never torn
nor stained and we never
have those American-sitcom
arguments about who shrunk what
and everything's good, everything's great

I just drop it off and pick it up.

jumped

my shoes are booted
out the side door
to jump
jumping spores
that stick in the rosemary
beneath spider webs
gathering beneath the roof
while pasta is stirred
beneath a light in the range hood
that glows fossil-yellow

so warm it's like a blanket
with invisible stitches
that cover the boiling water
which can't help but jump too
                and the speakers
they don't really jump at all
instead they hop
on the spot
and we can spot the
digital click
of electric-blue numbers

though we neither of us jump
while we wait
for the yellow pasta to go nearly white
beneath the white
and yellow light.

a table set for thousands

I will keep sucking poetry out of small things

out of stones, colours, seasons
words left behind
on ice
and roads
slick with black

I will draw it up with fingers spread at midnight
plunge my head into shadow
and fish out
the grey stuff
rearrange
until it fits on the page

I will hurl it up to cook in summer skies
knock down bits of blue
to fall like broomsticks in a storm

I will unwrap it on a table set for thousands
divide pieces
of a stolen alphabet

I will then search for more:

at archaeological digs, uncover it in frescos
beautiful and chipped

after gigs in cars for the long drive home,
find it squashed between a magazine
and the glare of headlights

outside front steps where so many boots
have made marks
sizes 8, 13, 10, 9, 8 again

in seconds before the telephone is answered
drop everything
go to it

even

in lines
waiting for stamps,
imagine it on my tongue.

concrete buttons

the street was always a flat division
between my bed and the cemetery.
the mown grass of our front yard,
twenty-something metres from
weeds round the tombstones, never worried me
for some reason. perhaps it was the makeshift
cricket pitch with its green-bin wicket,
where it stood between me, the ghosts and their leathery hands.
maybe it was the stunts, my little brother
standing on his BMX seat with arms spread wide,
or my own blue bike with back-pedal brakes
that left fish tails and dust everywhere, at least until
they sealed the road. it probably never bothered me,
because my nightmares
were not of shivering skeletons
crossing a blade-white street at night,
but of things much more human. from the elm tree
I would look down on concrete buttons of death,
and see with nothing but a child's eyes.

the colour purple

beside the river is a lost set piece
from *The Wizard of Oz*,
purple wildflowers
cover the paddock and bees
seem a little lazy,
their take-offs
hardly stir the pollen

the cows are like bold statues,
they do not even chew
much less swat at flies

and in the centre is a grass patch
as if some giant insomniac
had finally met his rest,
in the form of tiny flowers
with faces raised to the sun.

mythical

over a hundred years or more
shops and gelati
have crept closer to the Trevi Fountain

we queue for flavours
mythical,
not exactly sticking out
but hardly blending in.

the owner sings
and grins and holds the beat
as he slaps the counter,
tourists clap along
and my wife holds back a smile
when she orders
fragola, menta, vangilia
telling me afterwards
what he was really singing.

in the supermarket
we hunt for band-aids
and tissues
but neither can be found amongst
the aisles of olive oil or aprons
of patient shelving staff.

later, in the Sistine chapel,
the gaping mouths of hundreds
have recirculated all the air
so we make an escape

to Saint Peter's Square
where we shoot
the requisite photos

and as we smile for one another
a weight falls away

it's tangible, almost edible

finally we're invisible to our pasts
and in the split second
of each digital click
our joy is preserved, protected
by millions of 1s and 0s

where
we become two people
in the sun
beside a fountain
on the cobblestones
smiling.

tiger-shells

the beach has that
just-ironed look,
where the water
has smoothed
everything out
and made a
sloping tabletop
for the footprints
of lovers, they
last for hours
and the hopes that
go with them
overflow when
the tide returns
and tiger-shells
become scales
cast from sleeping
water-dragons.

things without beds

grey sneaks over netball courts
with black nets against
an orange glow, the sun has
infected the sky
and it's up to my lungs
to filter out
smoke from a controlled burn
and the merry home-fires of autumn

lights from lounge rooms
leak onto front lawns
and cast carnivalesque shadows
over things without beds,
wading pools
chew toys
and even Batman
sinking into a green Gotham

the footpath is unusually long
and dusk very short.

slow to get there

the new year starts
with a documentary on Stax
and Otis blowing them away
at Monterey

the doors and windows are open
but there's no breeze,
just more and more heat
as if the sun had hidden it
beneath the earth for later
and now mocks the moon,
now puts a heavy hand on my chest,
where I have sunk into the couch
like the slowest of shipwrecks.

tv torch song

so you sing to me still
but your voice is no longer
the not-quite-in-tune magic
of garage bands in summer

no longer the hum of a fisherman
coming home
after sleeping in brine
for months and dreaming of yellow fins
and a calm sea

no more the happy chatter of cafes
where people make plans
and laugh
and keep warm
when it rains outside

no more the gentle rustle
of a couple spreading jam on toast
each morning
and who take their time
with the paper
as you and I can no longer do.

lemon-yellow waltz

tonight I am waltzing a tomorrow
of lemon juice squirted onto
fish and chips, of bare feet
negotiating a minefield of prickles,
a day that slips right out of a Disney storyboard
and into this frost-bitten house

and when I wake
there may be a glimmer of it left
between the floorboards,
imprints where our smiles rested
and we fell sleep
without closing the windows.

stamped flat stamped

in my office between classes
I rage at flat things: the sea,
the land, the hard, flat dollar coin
and all its friends,
the road too short by far
and my feet, fingernails and thumbs
sleeping, none of them wings
I rage at the flat things
until my voice is stamped flat
stamped like the stamp of a soldier's liberating
boot; I rage until all my dreams are flat
I rage so quietly that animals come close
I rage so well that people congratulate me
I rage so far that distant mummies wake in
their glass cabinets, I rage at the rainbow slinky
just because it sits at my desk
I rage so that you notice and go away
I rage at flat things like the paper kipple
growing over me, I rage at words I cannot fix
I rage so deep that Hades lets Persephone go back
for more flowers and I rage so much that
it flattens my soul, now like a leaf
as it turns in the breeze,
and no one left to chase it.

man about town

who turns up to every party
late and slow
and seeks the bar
with an anteater for a face

who shakes but does not dance
who barely keeps sentences together
but instead leaves them
spread out between mouths
like washing hanging
on string between
old buildings in Europe

who makes up every cent
he's ever earned, who tears tissues
with earthy fingers
and fills the salad bowl with
the smell of rats

who is found hugging a pot plant
after the music stops,
who does not want to go home
and tried to eat every handshake

who wears American
highway-cop sunglasses and passes
out on the couch
between conversations, whose
pants come with black-hole pockets
for small change and fivers

who hits on girls in posters
and leaves lichen-like drool
on fluffy pillows

who is found the next morning
in the stairwell, stinking of the grave
and undergoing a terrible chrysalis
and twitching.

leather cocoon

on back roads headlights bore into her skull
and the quiet is new, as if everyone
had just gone to bed.
beside her, emptiness comes
from the passenger seat
and spreads into the fields
instead of the other way around.
jagged clouds pool in the moon's bowl
and the hours clog up behind her,
holding back the dawn.
she does not want to stop;
not for red things, not for memories
not for the phone in its leather cocoon
and especially not for tomorrow.
in fact, tomorrow cannot come,
she is not about to end a film
she is not some Marion Crane substitute
and the engine is strong, like a bull
or a thousand hooves in unison.

windstorm

we switched the heater off
a couple of hours ago
and I'm listening to the wind
roar around the room, outside
it's pushing against the weatherboard,
dragging bad memories with it.
it feels like no one could possibly
be happy out there.
not with all that awful
silence beneath the wind – it's all I can hear:
the glow of TVs in our street
smoke from chimneys, the neighbour
slamming a door and the cat snooping round gutters,
but no sounds. it's ridiculous, you're
only a room and a half away
but I feel alone, cut off from everything,
as if I could scream your name and
still the wind would erase me. I'm afraid
now, that you aren't telling me what you want,
that you're folding up your dreams, very neatly now
and slipping them into a card that could fit into any box
and I'm afraid I might pack them away in a rush
to get to my own, and that you'd love me
too much to make a sound.

ridges in the skin

it's doubtful that the sour woman
in the gelato shop
was in a mood
because of the thousands
of Capuchin monks
and poor Romans
buried across the street

she'd be used to looking
across to the doors

where five chambers
of pelvic bones
vertebrae and shoulder blades
in seven-foot cages
wait

and then a small chapel
with not even a knuckle bone

where the Mass will wait
until we tourists
have stumbled back
to our warm hotels
with slack faces
and a lingering chill,
very much aware of the marrow
beneath our skin.

things get better

I am sorting pencils in grass,
trying to use just one or two colours
to describe a land
waiting for rain so sweet
that it sticks to everything.

you take mint from its pot
with small scissors
and go back into the house,
music comes through the fly screen
and you sing while you cook.

you steal a boat

and I'll learn to navigate
by the stars
even if I have to cheat

the sea will be bruised
from the keel
but keep us going anyway

and the moon will
stay up on coffee
to make sure we land ok

and we'll in no way
envy the universe
for its light years of loneliness.

a hunk of tomorrow

morning was off
without your face it wasn't right
only my pillow
against the wall, red, the one hint of colour
in a house that we cleaned
a dozen times and left

> a pint of my blood in the garden
> and a black ball of resentment
> that slipped from the removal truck,
> shattering on the road
> where the ghosts of lawn clippings
> gathered in tiny remembrances
> that I imagined
> meant something

and we got out just in time to save your lungs
from another winter with coal dust
lining up to line your insides
with brown lines of sick
digging at your lifelines in palms
I didn't hold enough
screaming along the freeway after a late shift
car wheels – angels of grip! how well they
did whatever good engineering does,
and every time, I unlocked
the door after locking the gate
with white hands blue with chill
and walked in to see you, still awake
on the couch

I couldn't rupture the stillness
of the park across the road,
where spider webs ruled over visitors
and fog worked overtime
I could not invade, colonial with thin shoes
and lurid camera, capturing everything
I didn't care to leave to memory, bludgeoning
the shallow stream with its hard lens

and all that time, we barely photographed ourselves
better to forget, I suppose
now that we're in a sunnier place,
warm as a new coffee ring
or coats built for northern-hemisphere Christmases

better to forget, I know
the faces we wore then
and the future we inched toward,
faces that we could not clean of desperation
or maybe stubbornness, or whatever was left
        maybe we didn't forget
        after all
      still thankful at least
    still in a place where being still
    isn't so bad – like a crocodile
    waiting to get a hunk of tomorrow
    do something good with it.

one of the townsfolk

despite our closeness
after all the hours I've spent
at its feet
from childhood with sticky fingers
& wide pupils
to today, sneering at it from the couch
but still unable to switch it off
for good,
it waits
making no overtures
from plastic feet,
so still but still so predatory;
the remote, its sly little
Puck
its patience like an old, desert stone
waiting for rain.
it knows I will push, press
& stab at it with lazy fingers
circling
in an almost stoned
fishbowl dance
& I wonder what the television gives me

not just the pleasant cut-outs
of the sitcom & their dependability
being so utterly unlikely
to change,
nor is it shameful joy
beamed in via predictable
celebrity-failures
or even the news
when all I seem to want is mild weather,
& so if I'm not David
then I'm one of the squashed townsfolk
& I know that whatever resistance
I put up
is hardly going to wrap up a Western
or save planet earth.

particle detectors

goodnight
I'll say it over a green, hummed lullaby
to the daughter I imagine we'll have
knowing it will be but
the thinnest sound of comfort

knowing that no one will be able
to guarantee anything
not like saying
sweet dreams
and then chasing them down the next day

wondering if when you grow up
all the brightest sunshine will be swallowed
by thick safety boots
and the nervous clicking
of particle detectors lined up
in absolute mockery
of ice-cream trucks and Greensleeves.

snow

I threw a precious thing into the sea
and it sunk
into green weeds
and the red skin of sunbathers
did not bring Christmas to mind,
despite December
at full steam ahead

> I was not at home, waiting for presents
> eyes half-closed
> and snow on early morning TV,
> the chapped faces of Englishmen
> doing something Dickensian
> and me just unwrapping and imagining,
> having no idea about the existence
> of another hemisphere.

yellows

the city worries. its streets fill like ants before rain. shopping bags shackle. the wind rustles taxis. roads are liquorice chewed, spat into lines. wheels hijack space, stray leaves take on thuggish cigarette butts in gutters. ring-pulls hitchhike. twenty-foot women skyscrape, sell, sell, sell. lights remain tight lipped. 'closed' signs are never circles. glass cools. silver sprinkles the hats, horn notes fight through the ragged tap dance of trams. alleys leak. fast food yellows everything.

a ripening

through the window
at dusk
in the cold
I see a television half the size of a wall,
it blasts through lace curtains
and it's nothing like
when I was younger and the glow
from smaller boxes barely
made it outside.

in the supermarket
a memory of mango drifts across the aisles
and the self-service lane disappears
in its ripening

I have spent a long time waiting for the sun
to cross the sea
and dust everything at last
with its blinding footsteps,
show me
now
what has been so hard
to see.

twenty-thousand heartbeats

your umbrella doesn't open
all that well
our guide laughs, asking was it
purchased in Napoli?

into the city we go
with just enough rain
to darken Pompeii's streets,

the memory of washing
drying against orange
buildings
disappearing in an instant

the size of the place hits us

and we try to imagine the moment
twenty-thousand heartbeats
turned to stone.

Saint Mark's Square

from our train the few towers of Venice
float
guarding
the edge of the world,
holding back all the space
left over from old maps, when the world
just ran out

stopped
in a massive, continent-sized waterfall.

Piazza San Marco is ankle-deep in pigeons
and their leavings,
jazz bands
sneak into the drinks
and coat the yellow
tablecloths

and though we don't sit down

we eventually have to stop,
as people invariably halt
to stare up at bronze, replica horses
and unhook
their jeep-like cameras
right in the middle of the flow

and it is only later when we are on our way
out
that it doesn't
that it shouldn't matter

and the square goes *hush*
as sunlight melts on the Bell Tower
and Gabriel is set to blazing.

www.ingramcontent.com/pod-product-compliance
Lightning Source LLC
Chambersburg PA
CBHW070931080526
44589CB00013B/1476